SAVE OUR PLANET

Perritos/Dogs

Beagles/Beagles

por/by Jody Sullivan Rake

Traducción/Translation: Dr. Martín Luis Guzmán Ferrer
Editor Consultor/Consulting Editor: Dra. Gail Saunders-Smith

Consultor/Consultant: Jennifer Zablotny, DVM
Member, American Veterinary Medical Association

Capstone
press

Mankato, Minnesota

Pebble is published by Capstone Press,
151 Good Counsel Drive, P.O. Box 669, Mankato, Minnesota 56002.
www.capstonepress.com

1 2 3 4 5 6 13 12 11 10 09 08

Library of Congress Cataloging-in-Publication Data
Rake, Jody Sullivan.
    [Beagles. Spanish & English]
    Beagles / por Jody Sullivan Rake = Beagles / by Jody Sullivan Rake.
    p. cm. — (Pebble. Perritos = Pebble. Dogs)
    ISBN-13: 978-1-4296-2382-7 (hardcover)
    ISBN-10: 1-4296-2382-9 (hardcover)
    1. Beagle (Dog breed) — Juvenile literature. I. Title. II. Series.
SF429.B3R3518 2009
636.753'7 — dc22   2008001250

Summary: Simple text and photographs present an introduction to the beagle
    breed, its growth from puppy to adult, and pet care information — in both
    English and Spanish.

Note to Parents and Teachers

The Perritos/Dogs set supports national science standards related
to life science. This book describes and illustrates beagles in
both English and Spanish. The images support early readers in
understanding the text. The repetition of words and phrases helps
early readers learn new words. This book also introduces early
readers to subject-specific vocabulary words, which are defined
in the Glossary section. Early readers may need assistance to read
some words and to use the Table of Contents, Glossary, Internet
Sites, and Index sections of the book.

Table of Contents

Tabla de contenidos

4

Super Sniffers

Beagles like to sniff.
They have a good
sense of smell.

Buenísimos para olfatear

A los beagles les encanta
oler todo. Tienen un buen
sentido del olfato.

Some beagles work at airports. They sniff bags for unsafe items.

Algunos beagles trabajan en los aeropuertos. Olfatean las maletas para encontrar artículos peligrosos.

From Puppy to Adult

Beagle puppies are very curious. They learn about the world by sniffing everything.

De cachorro a adulto

Los cachorritos beagles son muy curiosos. Aprenden a conocer el mundo olfateando todo.

Beagle puppies drink
milk from their mothers.
They grow quickly.

Los cachorros beagle toman
leche de sus madres.
Crecen rápidamente.

Adult beagles are small dogs. They are a little taller than one stair.

De adultos los beagles son perros pequeños. Son un poco más altos que un escalón.

Taking Care of Beagles

Beagles have short fur.
Owners should brush
their beagles often.

Cómo cuidar a
los beagles

Los beagles tienen pelo
corto. Sus dueños deben
cepillarlos a menudo.

Beagles are full of energy.
Owners should walk their
beagles every day.

Los beagles tienen muchísima
energía. Sus dueños deben
pasearlos cada día.

17

Beagles are thirsty after exercise. They need water and food every day.

Los beagles tienen sed después de hacer ejercicio. Necesitan agua y comida todos los días.

Beagles love sniffing and playing. Beagles are great pets.

A los beagles les encanta olfatear y jugar. Los beagles son unas excelentes mascotas.

Glossary

curious — wanting to learn and investigate, interested in new things

energy — the ability to work and play for a long time, not getting tired easily

sense — a way of knowing about one's surroundings; seeing, hearing, touching, tasting, and smelling are the five senses.

sniff — to breathe in through the nose for smelling

Internet Sites

FactHound offers a safe, fun way to find Internet sites related to this book. All of the sites on FactHound have been researched by our staff.

Here's how:

1. Visit *www.facthound.com*
2. Choose your grade level.
3. Type in this book ID **1429623829** for age-appropriate sites. You may also browse subjects by clicking on letters, or by clicking on pictures and words.
4. Click on the **Fetch It** button.

FactHound will fetch the best sites for you!

Glosario

curioso — querer aprender e investigar, interesarse por las cosas nuevas

la energía — la habilidad de trabajar y jugar durante mucho tiempo, no cansarse fácilmente

olfatear — respirar por la nariz para oler

el sentido — manera de saber que es lo que nos rodea; la vista, el oído, el tacto, el gusto y el olfato son los cinco sentidos.

Sitios de Internet

FactHound te brinda una manera divertida y segura de encontrar sitios de Internet relacionados con este libro. Hemos investigado todos los sitios de FactHound. Es posible que algunos sitios no estén en español.

Se hace así:

1. Visita *www.facthound.com*
2. Elige tu grado escolar.
3. Introduce este código especial **1429623829** para ver sitios apropiados a tu edad, o usa una palabra relacionada con este libro para hacer una búsqueda general.
4. Haz un clic en el botón **Fetch It**.

¡FactHound buscará los mejores sitios para ti!

23

Index

adults, 13
eating, 11, 19
fur, 15
milk, 11
owners, 15, 17

pets, 21
puppies, 9, 11
size, 13
smell, 5
water, 19

Índice

dultos, 13
agua, 19
cachorros, 9, 11
comer, 11, 19
dueños, 15, 17

leche, 11
mascotas, 21
oler, 5
pelo, 15
tamaño, 13

Editorial Credits

Martha E. H. Rustad, editor; Katy Kudela, bilingual editor; Adalín Torres-Zayas, Spanish copy editor; Juliette Peters, designer; Jo Miller, photo researcher; Scott Thoms, photo editor

Photo Credits

Corbis/William Gottlieb, 16; Elite Portrait Design/Lisa Fallenstein-Holthaus, 14; Index Stock Imagery/Myrleen Cate, 20; Kent Dannen, 8, 10, 12; Lynn M. Stone, 4; Photo Researchers Inc./Renee Lynn, 18; Ron Kimball Stock/Ron Kimball, cover; Unicorn Stock Photos/Gary Randall, 1; USDA Photo by Ken Hammond, 6